Original title:
Behind the Living Room Curtains

Copyright © 2025 Creative Arts Management OÜ
All rights reserved.

Author: Jasper Montgomery
ISBN HARDBACK: 978-1-80587-189-7
ISBN PAPERBACK: 978-1-80587-659-5

Sentiments Woven in Time

Dust bunnies dance on the floor,
Hidden tales of memories galore.
Cats plot mischief, just out of sight,
As chairs conspire to hold them tight.

Old records spin a tune too loud,
While socks play hide-and-seek, quite proud.
A coffee cup, chipped but sincere,
With secrets to whisper, ever near.

The Radius of Solace

Cushy cushions hold their breath,
As we debate who's next in death.
The plants all gossip, leaves aglow,
About our love for snacks in tow.

A lamp's bright light, an awkward flair,
Supports our laughter, fills the air.
With every secret shared and sighed,
The radius grows, our hearts collide.

The Serenity of Familiar Walls

Walls listen closely, tales unfold,
In each crack, a laughter bold.
The clock ticks slowly, mocking us,
As we munch popcorn and discuss.

Framed pictures giggle, memories stored,
Of trousers shrunk and pets adored.
The remote's lost, we hunt in pairs,
Beneath the chaos, love it bears.

Eclipsed Glances of Connection

Eyes darting through draped displays,
A game of peekaboo that stays.
The dog plots pranks with every bark,
While kids declare the living room a park.

Laughter erupts, the echoes ring,
With each misstep, more chaos to bring.
In cozy chaos, we find our glee,
As glances weave a tapestry.

Daylight and Hidden Dreams

A cat in pajamas, curled up tight,
Dreams of tuna, oh, what a sight!
The sun spills in, a silly dance,
Birds outside, who took that chance?

Grandma's slippers, two sizes wide,
A peekaboo dance, she won't abide.
Chasing shadows, on the floor,
She yells, 'Expecting guests? No more!'

Conversations in the Quiet Nook

The sofa whispers secrets low,
To the coffee mug, who seems to know.
'What's that? A sandwich in the glovebox?'
'These crumbs aren't mine, don't be a fox!'

The old clock ticks with perfect cheer,
Interrupting thoughts, but who can hear?
A rogue sock sneaks under the chair,
'Take me instead!' it mutters, 'I swear!'

Reflections of the Human Heart

Mirrors laugh at the folks they see,
Flattering features—Oh, woe is me!
Through the glass, all dreams collide,
Pajama parties, we won't hide.

A fork in the salad, or maybe a spoon,
Together we dine, and waltz under the moon.
Laughter echoes, we spill like wine,
Our quirks combined make the best punchline!

Wanderings Through Domestic Landscapes

Dust bunnies keep their secrets well,
In the corners, stories they tell.
Bravely they march, what a parade,
'We're cleaning up!' they all have said!

The fridge hums a merry tune,
Leftover pizza dreaming of noon.
Oven mitts with a tale to share,
'That casserole? A daring affair!'

Shades of Stillness

A cat sprawls, dreaming wide,
A sofa is its pride.
The world outside may be loud,
Inside, we're snug and proud.

The plants lean in to hear,
What secrets drift from near.
With a sneeze, curtains sway,
As dust bunnies dance and play.

Secrets tucked within seams

A sock lost without a trace,
Beneath the couch, it found a space.
The remote, a long-lost friend,
With its buttons, we pretend.

The cushions giggle at the news,
Of crumbs and odd-shaped shoes.
A blanket fort will soon arise,
The cat's now king, to our surprise.

The Language of Shadows

When sunlight meets the floor,
A puppy sneaks by the door.
Shadows stretch and start to play,
As if whispering "stay, stay, stay."

The vase with flowers starts to lean,
As if it's part of the scene.
A lonely chair rolls its eyes,
At all the giggles and sighs.

Tides of Afternoon Light

The clock ticks, time does tease,
A snack break? Yes, please!
The curtains ripple and sway,
As if they're up for a play.

With giggles rolling like the tide,
A race to the sofa, we ride.
Afternoon shines, laughter's plight,
Each moment, a silly delight.

Moments Housed in Quietude

In the corner, a cactus sits,
Pointy and proud, never throwing fits.
Whispers dance with the dust in the air,
While the sofa sports a cat with flair.

A teacup trembles, filled to the brim,
As I ponder in silence, on a whim.
The clock ticks laughter, a jovial sound,
Embracing these moments, so tight and round.

The Dance of Awareness and Dreams

The cushions sway with a playful jig,
A ghost of popcorn does a little dig.
With every creak, the floorboards sing,
Of secrets woven in perky spring.

Sunlight pours in, it catches the dust,
In tiny twirls, a must-have for trust.
They say a sneeze can end the affair,
Yet here I am, a casual bear.

The Echo Chamber of Home

Echoes bounce off the fluffy rug,
With each chirp and chuckle, snug as a bug.
The lamp winks brightly, don't ask me how,
It's just here for laughs, living in the now.

The fridge hums softly, a rhythmic friend,
A chorus of snacks, our joy knows no end.
Bouncing shadows of all that we hold,
Whispers of chaos, yet never too bold.

A Palette of Fleeting Thoughts

Crayons scatter, a colorful mess,
Drawing thin lines of absurdity, I confess.
The walls giggle at my messy strokes,
A gallery of dreams, in quirky pokes.

The chair creaks like a wise old sage,
Holding stories, like a vibrant page.
Each tick of the clock, a chime of delight,
Brewing laughter in the quiet of night.

Light's Caress Through Woven Barriers

Sunshine peeks where it shouldn't dare,
Dust bunnies dance without a care.
My cat plots mischief, lurking sly,
While I sip coffee, just passing by.

The sofa holds secrets, cushions confide,
In the folds of fabric, all truths hide.
Remote controls wage a war of their own,
Lost in the cushions, forever alone.

The Enigma of Domestic Life

A plant sits tall, though he's barely alive,
Gnawing on snacks, I take a dive.
My laundry basket sings with clothes,
A fashion show only my dog knows!

The clock ticks loudly, plotting its scheme,
Time to vacuum—oh, what a dream!
Yet here I am, just slumped on the chair,
With popcorn kernels stuck in my hair.

Murmurs in the Half-Light

Shadows whisper behind the couch,
As I channel-surf, feeling like a slouch.
The fridge hums low, the dog gives a bark,
While the TV flickers, it's suddenly dark.

A sandwich calls out from the plate,
But laundry awaits; I procrastinate.
A kingdom of crumbs sprawled on the ground,
My snack-time throne where laughter is found.

Tales Hidden in Soft Shadows

The dust motes swirl in graceful dance,
Caught in glimpses of a half-hearted glance.
The coffee table holds a mystery or two,
As stray socks nod; do they know what to do?

Chairs squeak tales of relatives' fears,
While the floorboards creak with gossip from years.
In these quiet snippets, laughter takes flight,
As life unfolds softly, tucked out of sight.

Dreams Lurking Just Out of Sight

Whispers of the couch say, 'Don't be lazy,'
The cat rehearses its grand leap, oh so crazy.
A sock puppet chats with a duster proud,
While the TV watches, laughing out loud.

TV remotes hold secret fights,
Who gets the snacks? Oh, such delights!
Pillows plotting a take-over spree,
In the land of couch, who rules? Not me!

Stillness Framed by Fabric

Curtains sway, a dance of breeze,
Grandma's snores float by with ease.
The potted plant tells tales of woe,
To the lamp who just won't let it grow.

Dust bunnies form a tight-knit crew,
Planning their next great escape too.
Mothballs gossip, it's all rather wild,
While the carpet just rolls its eyes, beguiled.

Secrets We Share with Strangers

Neighbors peeking through the glass,
Are they shocked or just want to pass?
The fridge hums tunes of fridge magnet dreams,
While the chair sings softly of empty memes.

The vacuum plots for a coffee spree,
While the rug keeps the extraterrestrial decree.
And who knew that plants could spill such tea,
As they gossip with the curtain, oh so free!

Echoes of Laughter Behind the Glass

Laughter echoes off the walls so dear,
While a fish rolls its eyes, quite sincere.
The clock ticks time like it's in a race,
As shadows play tag, all over the place.

A crusty chair grumbles, does it feel old?
While pots and pans tell stories of bold.
Each chime and squeak a comedic tale,
In this cozy theater, where oddness prevails!

Conversations with the Unseen

Whispers float on the still air,
In a couch's warm embrace,
Pillow chats bring moments rare,
Laughter hides without a trace.

Invisible friends play their part,
Tickling truths that make us grin,
A sock's lost soul claims the heart,
While mischief brews beneath the skin.

Each dust particle, a jest so sly,
Curtains twitch with a knowing smile,
As life inside begins to fly,
Joy's mischief dances all the while.

Sippin' tea with a ghostly crew,
Chit-chat over crumbs of toast,
With every tale, a chuckle grew,
Who knew boredom could be a boast?

Fragments of Routine in Stillness

The clock strikes twelve, a ballet begins,
Socks tumble solo, they take the floor,
Dance partners slip, yet everyone wins,
Reality's zany, leave them wanting more.

The cat's on guard, with paws crossed tight,
As shadows play beneath the gleam,
A squirrel's heist within the night,
Turns each tiny space into a dream.

Crumbs underfoot tell tales divine,
Each snack run worthy of a cheer,
Home's delightful chaos intertwines,
As each odd moment draws us near.

Between the walls, hilarity reigns,
Where laughter finds a cozy nook,
A life that dances, free from chains,
Inside these frames, the quirks are hooked.

The Shield of Comfort Zones

The sofa's a fortress, soft and wide,
Where secrets bloom like wildflowers,
In laughter's arms, we all abide,
A place where time defies the hours.

Cereal bowls begin their reign,
As laughter spills, mix-ups abound,
Every mishap, a light-hearted gain,
In our cozy realm, joy is found.

Recliners hold our idle tales,
With snacks as bait, we spin delight,
In comfort's arms, no ship that sails,
Could ever break this funny night.

From the outside, we may appear bland,
But inside, the riot's a lively brother,
With high-fives and love; we make our stand,
In the warmth of walls, we don't smother.

Unraveling Threads of Normalcy

A rug's woven tales tell stories grand,
Of pranks and giggles that left their mark,
Each shifty glance, a fun-filled strand,
Where every norm dances in the dark.

Silly socks find their mismatched match,
In playful puns and raucous grins,
Through every stitch, an unseen patch,
Connection grows where laughter spins.

Chairs squeak in rhythm to life's sweet tune,
While corners host spontaneous jams,
Like a well-oiled machine's comical rune,
Making fun from the mundane reclams.

As curtains sway like a playful breeze,
The house reverberates with this wonderful cheer,
In the heartbeat of life, we find our ease,
With ordinary moments that bring us near.

A Portal to the Ordinary

A cat naps on a sunbeam,
The dog dreams of being spry,
While kids play hide and seek,
And the plants just watch and sigh.

The fridge hums a silly tune,
The clock ticks like a metronome,
Dishes stack in a daring tower,
As old socks find a new home.

Laptops buzz and screens dazzle,
While crumbs scatter like lost dreams,
Someone snorts at a bad joke,
And laughter spills from bursting seams.

Amid the chaos, life unfolds,
Like a movie without a plot,
Every glance behind the drapes,
Is a scene that hits the spot.

The Curtain's Conspiracy

The curtains whisper secrets low,
Of dust bunnies playing charades,
They giggle when the cat stumbles,
And cheer for the circus parades.

Pillows plot a fluffy revolt,
As snacks conspire to escape,
Remote controls vanish on cue,
In this comical landscape.

Toys hold council in the night,
Making plans for their big debut,
Socks sneak out on daring quests,
In this comedy so true.

Laughter echoes off the walls,
In bright colors that shine and glint,
Every daily mischief caught,
In the fabric and in the lint.

Whimsy Amidst the Threads

A sock puppet shows up for tea,
While the vacuum plots a race,
The rug rolls its eyes at the mess,
As the clock keeps up the pace.

Cushions bounce like excited kids,
Jokes fly through the air with zest,
The room is alive with chatter,
In this haven, we feel blessed.

Mismatched shoes discuss their dreams,
As crayons make art on the floor,
Leftover snacks tell silly tales,
In our whimsical folklore.

Every corner holds a wink,
And every smile's a spark of glee,
In this cozy little world of ours,
Where humor sets the spirit free.

Veils of Familiarity

The curtains sway to a soft beat,
As tea leaves dance in their cup,
The toaster pops with a funny grin,
And the microwave says, 'What's up?'

Dish towels gossip about the food,
While chairs squeak with a wise old sound,
Every item is a character here,
In this play, tightly wound.

Puppies wagging their fluffy tails,
While the remote rolls to hide in glee,
This is where our hearts find home,
In this joyful family spree.

Each glance shared through the fabric,
Is a wink, a nod, a knowing glance,
In this space of relatable quirks,
Life's a laugh, and we all dance.

Whispers of the Afternoon Light

The sun spills gold on the floor,
Cats stretch out, dreaming of more.
Pillow forts built with pride,
Little spies in a cushy hide.

Chips and giggles float through the air,
Who knows what's hiding under the chair?
A sock puppet's plotting a scheme,
While kids concoct their wildest dream.

Secrets of the Draped World

A curtain twitches with secret glee,
What are they whispering? Let's see!
Dust bunnies giggle, they hide so well,
In the fabric, they weave their spell.

The remote control rolls, a thief on the run,
Stealing the spotlight, oh what fun!
A marshmallow fight erupts with a boom,
As laughter spills from the cozy room.

Shadows Danced on Fabric

Shadows play tag on the couch,
A rabbit hops, pretending to slouch.
The floorboards creak in a silly tune,
While the lamp casts a whimsical moon.

A sock sneaks out for a daring quest,
To find its mate, oh what a jest!
The goldfish chuckles, flitting about,
"Who's the real star? We've no doubt!"

Tapestries of Hidden Stories

Under the throws, secrets conspire,
Doodle drawings that never tire.
Mom's old sweater, stained with love,
Holds memories, as if from above.

A game of charades with pillows in play,
While the dog snores loud, in the fray.
A spontaneous dance, twirling around,
With giggles and claps, oh, what a sound!

The Art of Stillness

In the quiet of the day,
A cat sprawls without a care.
The fridge hums its gentle song,
And I wonder if it's aware.

The clock ticks loud, a friend or foe,
Each second sneaks, then runs away.
The dust bunnies have a show,
With popcorn made of yesterday.

The couch is witness to my plight,
It knows all my snacks, my late-night bites.
Who knew stillness could invite,
So many thoughts that take their flights?

In this sanctuary of soft repose,
Tomorrow's worries, here, I expose.
Yet in this calm, hilarity grows,
With a wave of laughter, I suppose.

A Canvas of Calm

A blanket fort stands proud and tall,
Its walls of fluff, a cozy hall.
With crayons scattered on the floor,
A masterpiece awaits, to scrawl.

The cat critiques my work of art,
With a yawn, it plays its part.
While chips and dip adorn the scene,
A culinary abstract, quite avant-garde.

The curtains sway, like dancers free,
They beckon thoughts, quiet, carefree.
As I sip my tea, it's plain to see,
Adventure lives through daydreams' spree.

So here I sit, a painter bold,
With stories woven, yet untold.
With laughter echoing, secrets unfold,
In this canvas of calm, life feels gold.

Soliloquies of Soothing Light

The sun spills gold across the floor,
While socks escape from the closet door.
A dance of shadows, light takes flight,
In this playhouse of soft delight.

The clock's face yawns with time's embrace,
While dust motes swirl in a chase.
The slippers giggle, at mischief's call,
And I, the audience, enjoy it all.

The fridge reveals surprise delights,
A half-eaten cake shows me its bites.
In this warm glow of fading day,
Life serves up humor, come what may.

As shadows lengthen, tales are spun,
On quirky days, we laugh and run.
In the heart of calm, we find our fun,
With light as our guide, we're never done.

Threads of Comfort and Kindness

A threadbare couch is home to dreams,
Where laughter bursts at the seams.
Each stitch tells tales of times gone by,
In cozy corners, we laugh and sigh.

The TV drones a rerun show,
While popcorn takes flight, a buttery snow.
We giggle at plots, so absurd, yet true,
Crafting our moments, just me and you.

The lamp flickers, a warm embrace,
Casting shadows that dance with grace.
In the fabric of this simple night,
We weave our stories, fun and light.

So let's toast to naps and snacks galore,
To moments that leave us wanting more.
In this tapestry of warmth we explore,
With threads of comfort stitched at the core.

The Orchestra of Evening Twilight

The sun bows down, the shades unite,
As shadows dance, oh what a sight!
Cats on the prowl, they're on the chase,
A parade of giggles, a wild embrace.

The crickets tune their tiny strings,
While children laugh, and joy takes wing.
A dog plays fetch with a broomstick tight,
In this grand play of the soft twilight.

The couch has secrets, cushions hide,
Busted popcorn dreams, laughter applied.
A make-believe band, the pillows beat,
Each plop and flop, an evening treat.

The moon peeks in, its head a swirl,
As socks get lost in a curious whirl.
The twilight concert ends with cheer,
In this funny world, we hold so dear.

Where Everyday Wonders Flourish

The kettle whistles, tea's in sight,
While mismatched socks enjoy their flight.
A chair spins 'round, an impromptu ride,
In the land of quirks, we take great pride.

A flower pot speaks in silent glee,
It shows the cat, who's in on the spree.
Dust bunnies whisper, secrets they share,
As we stumble through moments, unaware.

Chasing thoughts through a coffee mist,
The remote is lost, can't be missed.
Jokes are traded over simple meals,
In this quirky world, wonder reveals.

The dishes dance in the bubbly foam,
While the tablecloth dreams of a new home.
Everyday magic, a daily rush,
Here hilarity thrives, in a joyful hush.

The Comfort of Unwritten Stories

A notebook lay with pages bare,
It waits for tales of debonair.
Pencil grins, the eraser sighs,
As laughter hides in thin disguise.

The lamp flickers, casting shade,
A sock puppet schemes, a masquerade.
Whispers fly 'cross the silent room,
While night blooms with its playful plume.

A family feud o'er the last slice pie,
The stubborn dog lets out a sigh.
Sticky notes dance on the fridge's door,
In this unwritten, who needs more?

With blankets piled, we drift and float,
A car's just a box, a cap of coat.
Stories yet told, but laughter bound,
In this cozy chaos, joy is found.

Pockets of Stillness

Inside the house, the clock stands still,
Its ticking giggles, a timeless thrill.
A squirrel peeks in, with nut in hand,
Whispers of nature, oh so grand.

Blankets drape like clouds of fluff,
Hiding strange treasures, life is tough.
A rogue shoe dances on the floor,
Soliciting chuckles, begging for more.

Cups chatter gently, tea time's here,
Beneath the laughter, a heartfelt cheer.
Corners hold secrets, in different hues,
Waiting for moments, we might not choose.

The fridge hums softly, a lullaby,
As plates spark joy, with food piled high.
In this quiet nook, laughter fills space,
Our funniest tales, in hidden embrace.

Threads of Unforgotten Echoes

Worn-out curtains sway and dance,
As I catch the neighbors' glance.
They think I'm busy, lost in thought,
But really, it's gossip I have sought.

The dog next door, he barks so loud,
He thinks he's part of the crowd.
I wave to friends who cannot see,
As they sip coffee, unaware of me.

Dust motes swirl like secrets shared,
While laughter fades, no one cared.
I'm peeking through this fabric veil,
With stories told that never fail.

Oh, to be a fly on the wall,
To hear the echo of each call.
With humor bubbling just like stew,
In the tales I weave, all true for you!

The Gaze of Unseen Lives

Peering out with quirky schemes,
I watch my neighbors chase their dreams.
One wears socks with sandals bold,
A fashion statement never told.

A cat pounces, plots and curls,
While children spin in dizzy twirls.
Each life a play, a comic show,
And I'm the audience, here, below.

Muffins burn, with smoke a-scream,
Dad's on the phone, oh, what a dream!
Mom's rolling eyes, her antics wild,
Amidst the chaos, she's still a child.

From my post, the light shines bright,
Oh, how we revel in this sight!
Behind the scenes, the laughter rings,
Unseen lives with invisible strings.

Dissolving Sounds of Routine

The clock ticks loud, a comical sound,
As coffee spills, both hot and brown.
Children's laughter fills the hall,
While the cat performs a daring fall.

A neighbor shouts as the door slams tight,
Their daily bickering, a silly fright.
As I munch on yesterday's bread,
I giggle at the chaos ahead.

The phone rings twice, then silence flows,
Juggling chores in a silly prose.
With every clang and every clash,
Life dissolves in a comedic flash.

So here I sit, in comfy clothes,
Finding humor in what life bestows.
Each small drama, a pearl so bright,
Dissolving sounds, a pure delight.

Embraces in the Warmth of Home

In the cozy nook where I reside,
Stories linger, side by side.
A sofa naps, its cushions wide,
While clumsy feet dance with pride.

Bubbles in the sink, splashes and grins,
We wrangle ducks and rinse our sins.
Laughter echoes, what a sight,
As pets join in, igniting the night.

The fridge hums tunes of leftover cheer,
With mystery meals no one will hear.
While shadows play a game of hide,
In warmth of home, our hearts collide.

So here we gather, in this embrace,
With silly antics, we find our place.
In every corner, a tale unfolds,
In the warmth of home, our joy is bold.

The Mask of Familiar Faces

In a realm where laughter plays,
The cat wears glasses, quite a craze.
Dogs in ties debate the news,
While goldfish gossip, sharing views.

A chair pranks the sofa with a smile,
Every cushion plotting, with style.
Tick-tock goes the clock, in jest,
Who knew home could be such a fest?

At night when shadows start to creep,
The vacuum sings the tunes of sleep.
Fridge hums sweet lullabies so bright,
While pantry whispers secrets light.

Familiar faces in the fray,
Each corner holds a playful sway.
In this circus, all's a jest,
With the remote, we are all blessed.

Realm of Soft Shadows

In the realm where shadows roam,
Lamps dance like they've found a home.
The curtains wiggle to the beat,
As dust bunnies join in for a seat.

The sofa snores, a hearty sound,
While picture frames spin round and round.
Each twilight brings a new charade,
As we giggle at the masquerade.

Conversations held in whispers low,
Wink at the hall where echoes flow.
The rug plays tag with careless feet,
Every step—such humorous treat.

When bedtime stories start to fade,
The world transforms, excitement made.
Underneath the cloak of night,
Our silly truths come to the light.

Whispers of Everyday Epiphanies

The coffee pot breathes in delight,
As mugs exchange tales of the night.
A spoon sings songs of sugar sweet,
While the kettle taps its happy feet.

The toaster pops with unexpected cheer,
To announce breakfast is finally here.
A cereal box speaks of dreams,
Saying mornings bring the silliest schemes.

A couch confesses its favorite show,
As throw pillows join the lively row.
Remote control acts like a king,
In this realm, all objects sing.

By sunlight or the evening hue,
Every day brings something new.
With laughter hiding in each crack,
Home is where we let joy unpack.

Glimpses of Heartfelt Solitude

In corners Cozy, thoughts take flight,
A dust motes tango in the light.
The chair hums tunes of lazy dreams,
While cushions plot their crafty schemes.

The clock winks by, as minutes tease,
"Stay awhile, you'll never freeze."
A whimsical dance of silent bliss,
In solitude, a gentle kiss.

Each book on the shelf shares its lore,
Whispers of worlds beyond the door.
In the silence, chuckles ring,
As the cat narrates the oddest fling.

In these quiet moments, we find
Laughter wrapped in the heart and mind.
Life's little quirks, a treasure chest,
In solitude, we find our best.

The Soundtrack of Silence

The clock ticks loud, a band on strike,
While neighbors bicker, yet none take flight.
The cat's a critic, on the windowsill,
Gazing at the world, with a silent thrill.

Mismatched shoes parade on the floor,
Granting each step a dramatic encore.
Dust bunnies waltz, they're quite a sight,
In this quirky show, where wrong feels right.

The TV hums, a forgotten song,
While socks play tag, it won't be long.
Echoes of laughter, they float and sway,
In this odd little play, all night and day.

Curtains hide secrets, like notes unsent,
In a living room where the giggles are pent.
With a flick of the wrist, and a sneaky glance,
Life's a jest, given half a chance.

Fleeting Thoughts in Fleecy Haze

The sofa's plush, it swallows whole,
Whispers of dreams, in cushy control.
A snack left unattended, a con job spree,
As crumbs flood the corners like sneaky debris.

A cup of coffee tries to flirt,
With a distant plant, dressed in dirt.
Imaginary friends debate in the light,
Over whose turn it is to sleep tight.

The curtain flutters, a ghostly dance,
While the goldfish plans its big romance.
Is that a shadow or just my mind?
In this cozy chaos, we're all entwined.

Tickle the air, let smiles take flight,
In the haze of this room, everything's bright.
Chasing thoughts that drift like a breeze,
In a land where laughter does as it please.

The Glimmer of Daydreams

A pillow kingdom, where knights reside,
Waging war on weariness, in whimsical stride.
The fork sings tunes while waiting for cake,
As the fridge hums sweetly, for goodness' sake.

Cushions collide in a plush little fight,
While shadows do cartwheels, oh what a sight!
A stray balloon floats by with flair,
Enjoying the chaos, without a care.

Main course is mischief, with sides of chuckles,
As the coffee pot gurgles, and silently cuddles.
A twirling lamp drips light like confetti,
In this circus of moments, nothing's too petty.

With every peek through fabric dreams,
Life's a zany parade of giggles and schemes.
So toast to the antics, both grand and small,
Where laughter is king, and we're all at the ball.

Infinite Echoes of Ordinary Hours

A sock rebellion brews near the chair,
With one lone shoe playing solitaire.
The dishes debate, who'll get to dry,
In this raucous room where the quirks never die.

Chairs have opinions, they creak and moan,
While laughter wrestles for a warm throne.
Curtains leap like fish in a stream,
As sunlight doodles a whimsical dream.

The coffee pot murmurs a sleepy tune,
With spoons spinning tales of the man in the moon.
Here, echoes of mundane morph into plays,
As time takes a bow, and chaos parades.

In every tick, a mystery's spun,
In this realm where we play, there's no need to run.
So clap for the moments, the laugh lines, and cheer,
For in this sweet mess, life's brilliantly clear.

Fragments of Forgotten Dialogues

Whispers drift through fabric seams,
Like secrets buried in daydreams.
A sock puppet claims it's quite the star,
While the cat plots snacks from afar.

The goldfish nods with watery glee,
Eavesdropping on debates of tea.
A squirrel sneaks crumbs from the window,
As laughter stirs in a gentle crescendo.

Old magazines gossip, dust in the air,
Stories untold, no one seems to care.
An elbowed chair groans under the weight,
Of idle chatter, both mundane and great.

A broom leans in, listening tight,
To two chairs arguing about the night.
On the walls, shadows dance and prance,
Oh, the tales of a room's odd romance!

Hushed Stories in the Air

In corners where giggles dare to linger,
A daisy chain broken by a small finger.
The lamp chuckles, casting playful light,
As the puppy dreams of chasing the night.

Beneath the table, a world spins round,
Where imagination leaps, joy abounds.
The dust combines in a swirling waltz,
Binding the quirks—hey, no one faults!

The TV flickers, sharing bad jokes,
A sitcom laugh track, it provokes.
While the fridge hums sweet lullabies,
In soft tones that float like fireflies.

There's magic in every comical glance,
A cookie jar sings, "Come on, take a chance!"
In this realm where stories weave and play,
Hushed laughter echoes, come join the fray!

Lifetimes in a Single Gaze

A glance can spark a thousand tales,
Of lovers' quarrels and epic fails.
The couch sighs deep with old memories,
While the chair nods, as if in agree.

Nearby, a painting rolls its eyes,
Chronicling truths wrapped in white lies.
A dog snoozes, dreaming of space,
Chasing cosmic cats in a merry race.

The clock ticks slow, with a knowing wink,
As the world swirls on, and we rethink.
An airborne dust bunny takes flight,
Crashing into dreams born of pure delight.

Life unfolds in the silence we keep,
In knowing smiles, in laughter, in sleep.
Each gaze a window, a breather, a pause,
In this theater of life, we clap and we draw.

Curtains that Shield

Each fold protects a raucous cheer,
From rubber ducks that gather near.
A cushiony throne where giggles bloom,
Where even the shadows find space to loom.

The telephone eavesdrops, ever so sly,
On tales of green monsters that sigh.
Stuffed bears nod to secrets shared,
While the curtains blush, feeling bared.

A tangle of sneakers, a pile of socks,
Hide the chaos from nosy hawks.
The sofa's cushions hold pantomime plays,
Of kittens and cookies, in shadowy bays.

Muffled laughter rolls thick like pie,
As the dust motes tap dance and fly.
In this haven where nonsense finds reign,
Curtains that shield our quirks remain!

A Gallery of Fleeting Emotions

The cat pretends to be a spy,
Prowling the couch and hiding nearby.
While I sip tea, it makes a leap,
Catching shadows with a pounce so deep.

The clock ticks loud; it's quite the drum,
As I laugh at his silly, clumsy run.
He trips on socks, all curly and round,
In this art show, chaos is abound.

Guests arrive, and chaos reigns,
With misplaced cushions and tangled trains.
They wonder why the dog acts aloof,
As the cat takes aim from under the roof.

Haunted by crumbs from last night's snack,
A trail of popcorn leads to the back.
In this gallery, laughter paints the walls,
As I smile at the mayhem that calls.

Angles of Sunlit Reverie

Sunbeams slink through gaps to tease,
A dance of dust that floats with ease.
I smile at the antics the couch can yield,
As cushions soar, like laughter revealed.

The dog rolls over, a floppy mess,
While a squirrel steals crumbs, feeling blessed.
Laughter erupts from the corner chair,
As socks take flight through the sunlit air.

Family stories twist and bend,
With giggles that seem to never end.
The room is buzzing, a joyful hum,
Where snapshots live and puns become.

Outside, the world spins fast and loud,
But here, we bounce like bubbles unbowed.
A playful dream on this lazy day,
Where sun and silliness have their say.

Caught in the Frame of Life

The camera clicks, a moment snared,
With goofy faces that none have dared.
We strike a pose, all mismatched and bright,
While the dog yawns, stealing the spotlight.

Someone spills juice, oh what a mess!
We laugh it off, more silly than stress.
Each snapshot holds a treasure trove,
Of awkward smiles and funny stoves.

The kids are giggling, making a show,
While some dance like they're in slow-mo.
Each frame a story that bids to be seen,
Our living room's a movie screen.

So here we sit, wide grins on display,
In this misfit frame, we find our way.
Emotions flip like pancakes in flight,
Beaming with joy in the soft, warm light.

Unraveled Strings of a Cozy Existence

The knitting basket spills its yarn,
As cats entwine, oh what a charm!
A tangled mess of colors bright,
Where every twist brings pure delight.

I trip on sweaters, that much is true,
While laughter erupts with every 'boo!'
Lost in a world of fabric and play,
Where fibers of fun come out to stay.

From cups of tea to biscuits shared,
These are moments that we've all dared.
The clock keeps ticking, yet time suspends,
Laughter echoes where comfort blends.

So here's to the joy of catching stray threads,
A life stitched together, where chaos spreads.
With fuzzy socks and laughter's embrace,
In this cozy realm, we find our place.

The Space Where Silence Sits

In shadows soft, the dust bunnies play,
Beneath the couch, they brew their ballet.
While I sip tea, they dance with delight,
Whispering secrets, hidden from sight.

The wall clock ticks like a comedian's joke,
Each hour it chimes, pretending to poke.
I snicker aloud, as the cat takes a leap,
Chasing the echoes, into a dream deep.

Books in a pile, tales bursting to flee,
Waiting for someone to open and see.
Each title winks, with a curious charm,
"Read me," they plead, but I stay unarmed.

A tumble of socks, mismatched and proud,
Join in the giggles, a soft cotton crowd.
In this funny space, silence finds its seat,
While laughter lingers, playful and sweet.

Sunbeams and Hidden Dreams

Sunlight giggles through the parted shades,
Drawing curious shadows like playful parades.
Dust motes dance, like tiny jesters abound,
In this lighthearted realm, silliness is found.

With half-opened books, a pillow fort grows,
Where imaginations wander, and laughter flows.
An octopus pirate prepares for a raid,
As plush toys gather, their plans well-laid.

The chair squeaks like a character's quip,
While the table holds secrets, just waiting to slip.
Misfit socks giggle in their hiding place,
A sock puppet show, with a mission to brace.

In this sunny glow, dreams take their flight,
With every chuckle escaping the night.
Behind curtains drawn, the whimsy takes hold,
Where laughter is pure, and stories unfold.

Echoes from the Hearth

Crackling whispers float through the air,
The fireplace crackles with a mischievous flare.
Mismatched chairs plot their next scenario,
While the kitten climbs up, on a furry stereo.

Old photographs chuckle from dusty frames,
Each grin and gaze whispers ridiculous names.
A tangle of yarn sprawls like a bad art spree,
Purring like laughter, alive with glee.

The soup pot bubbles like gossip in stew,
While spoons try to dance, in a jazzy skew.
The smell of a mishap wafts through the space,
Uh-oh, was that dinner? Oh, what a disgrace!

In this warm nook, humor brews strong,
As echoes of laughter carry along.
Like a sitcom's punchline caught just off guard,
Life behind the flames is rarely hard.

Gazes Thwarted by Thread

Soft fabric flutters, like whispers unheard,
While curious critters plot mischief, undeterred.
Cats peek and pounce, tails twitching with glee,
Bounding through sunlight, oh, what a spree!

Threaded secrets hang from the window's embrace,
Every stitch tells stories with laughter and grace.
The gardener's hat, a crown for the queen,
With a splash of color, an unexpected sheen.

Stitching together the day's little pranks,
As the chair reclines, giving giggling thanks.
A parade of socks, mismatched and bold,
Delightfully bursting with tales to unfold.

With towels on hooks, all ready to cha-cha,
As suns painted orange dip low in the plaza.
In this world of thread, hearts skip with cheer,
Behind fabric and dream, joy draws ever near.

Echoes of the Unspoken

The cat leaps high, in chase of dust,
A tumbleweed of fur in playful thrust.
Neighbors argue over who will save,
The prize-winning tomato, oh what a grave!

A tea kettle sings, the water's a riot,
My socks mismatched — who'd dare to try it?
A sandwich waits, still fresh and neat,
While crumbs gather under the chair's seat.

Giggling kids roam the yard with flair,
Who knew a grasshopper would cause such despair?
With every giggle, the curtains sway,
Life's little dramas unfold at play.

Laughter bubbles up like brittle soda,
Why did Uncle Fred wear that dreadful coat-a?
Peeking from corners, a pet's sly plan,
Are you watching, or is it just the fan?

Glimpses of Moments Unfolding

The dog spots a squirrel, oh what a sight,
His antics to catch it bring pure delight.
The teapot trembles, a whimsical dance,
As I sip my tea, and give it a chance.

Kids with their cookies stacked up so high,
A tower of crumbs reaching up to the sky.
The parrot squawks truths no one believes,
While your "secret" is hidden behind the leaves.

Neighbors wave from an odd angle or two,
What strange tales could they possibly construe?
Their gossip wafts in like a warm breeze,
As I crack a grin, at the world's little tease.

Mismatched plates from lunch lay in a pile,
Did that fork really go missing a while?
With laughter nearby, you can feel the cheer,
Moments like these are treasures to hold dear.

The Soft Glow of Afternoon

Sunshine spills, a golden stream,
As shadows dance, it feels like a dream.
Cats curl up in a sunbeam's embrace,
While I twitch the curtains, hoping for grace.

A cheeky breeze makes papers take flight,
Chasing after them becomes pure delight.
Grandma's old stories echo in the air,
As giggles and whispers wander with flair.

Two kids race past, a challenge in tow,
Over the garden, their laughter will flow.
Hopscotch and chalk stains paint the path,
While I pretend to escape their math.

The ice cream truck's jingle climbs up the wall,
What joy it brings in that sugary sprawl.
With every scoop, the world fades away,
And for a brief moment, I wish I could stay.

Where Light Meets Shadow

Bumbling insects buzz with delight,
They dance in the sun, what a funny sight.
The blinds tilt just right, a theatrical play,
Where shadows jump and wiggle away.

The phone rings once, then twice in a row,
Will it be mom, or the neighbor, I don't know?
A whoopee cushion sets off a spree,
Laughter erupts, oh what glee!

Sunset paints the walls with playful hue,
Leaving me guessing just what to do.
Retreating to corners like shy little sprites,
As the day waves goodbye, igniting the nights.

In the quiet, whispers tickle my ear,
Are those voices I hear, or just winds drawing near?
With each creak of the floor, life's antics abound,
In a world where silliness endlessly surrounds.

The Palette of Everyday Life

A sock that sneaks from under the chair,
Dances in rhythm with dust in the air.
A cat on the couch, in a mighty pose,
Declares the cushions are now her throne, I suppose.

The refrigerator hums a tune so sweet,
While leftovers plot their quirky retreat.
A mystery snack lies under a lid,
With a note saying, 'Please eat me, I hid!'

The lamp flickers like it's got a joke,
Every time the old dog gives a poke.
A shoe with a story, lost at the door,
Is part of the fun in this home we adore.

The remote's a magician, it vanishes fast,
While laughter erupts, our moments are cast.
Colors and quirks paint our little space,
In this palette of life, there's joy in the chase.

Silhouettes at Dusk

Shadows of pets running wild in the night,
Creep on the wall, causing quite a fright.
A ghostly figure, is it a prank?
No, just a child, off to the tank.

With fingers like noodles, they reach for a snack,
Sneaking past parents to stage a small act.
Lamp post glow makes them dance like a sprite,
In our little theatre where no one is right.

The curtains flutter like they're in a race,
Masked by the dusk, a light-hearted chase.
A silhouette steps back to reveal a grin,
As chaos erupts with the neighbors' loud din.

At dusk, we laugh under midnight skies,
With shadows who giggle and wide-open eyes.
The silliness reigns as we settle for dreams,
Silhouetted in joy, or so it seems.

A Symphony of Unheard Laughter

In corners unseen, the giggles collide,
With cereal spills being their secret guide.
Toys in a chorus, they sing out of tune,
While guardians sigh, 'Oh, not this afternoon!'

The cat's ballad is one of pure sass,
Gracing the room with a dramatic pass.
As crumbs make a bed on the well-worn rug,
A munching symphony starts with a shrug.

The fridge takes a bow with a thud and a clank,
While snacks join the chorus, no room for a prank.
In silent uproar, our joy is profound,
An unheard laughter that bubbles all around.

The curtains may sway as the giggles grow louder,
While the clock thinks it's wise, but can't get prouder.
As bedtime approaches, the performance won't cease,
In a symphony of joy, our hearts find their peace.

Reflections on Worn Carpet

The carpet wears stories from ages of play,
Where spilled juice rivers became a bouquet.
Rug burns and laughter stitched into threads,
In the fabric of life, where joy never sheds.

Each stain tells a tale of daring delight,
Whispered secrets that slip through the night.
A jigsaw of footprints imprints our spree,
As we sprint to the fridge for some late-night tea.

Sunlight spills in, revealing the mess,
A conference of toys now in recess.
The dust bunnies giggle as they make their retreat,
While we plop down in laughter, clouding our feet.

In the worn-out mess, there's comfort galore,
Where every reflection is worth so much more.
The world may be hectic, but here it is grand,
In the tapestry woven by love's gentle hand.

Daydreams in Dusty Corners

In the corner, dust bunnies play,
Hosting parties by the break of day.
Chairs listen close to whispers near,
While couch potatoes cheer with beer.

The cat conducts, a grand meow,
As socks wander, lost, somehow.
The TV's gossip fills the room,
As crumbs plot under couch to bloom.

A lamp gossips with the old chair,
Sharing secrets of life laid bare.
The rug spins tales of feet grown sore,
As laughter echoes evermore.

The Veil of Everyday Life

Dishes stack like a tower high,
While dust participates in the pie.
Pants hang out to dry on hooks,
As neighbors peek with curious looks.

The fridge hums tunes of leftover pies,
While squirrels plot their dinner spies.
Mismatched socks waltz on the floor,
As brooms sweep away their encore.

The clock ticks loudly, full of cheer,
Reminding me my nap is near.
As tea brews tales of modern strife,
The day slips by, full of life.

Observations from Within

Through tinted panes, the world waits,
While curtains peek at chatted mates.
Half-formed thoughts drift 'round the room,
As dust motes dance in afternoon gloom.

A spider spins a web so fine,
Declaring it a dining line.
The remote hides, a sneaky queen,
In a kingdom that's rarely seen.

A wipe of crumbs turns into giggles,
As the blender hums and wiggles.
Cats judge the world from the sill,
While I plot out my next big thrill.

The Quietude of Domestic Places

The chair creaks softly, tired and wise,
As the dog dreams of pizza pies.
Walls keep secrets of laughter shared,
While plants scheme and plot, unprepared.

Mugs are stacked, a mini tower,
Cupcakes wait for their golden hour.
The rug's got stories from little feet,
And spills that just can't retreat.

A clock ticks humor in time's embrace,
While rubber bands engage in a race.
Through everyday sights, we laugh and sigh,
As the world spins on, just you and I.

Secrets Cradled in Fabric

Draped in colors soft and light,
Whispers gather, day and night.
Elbows poke and giggles burst,
In threads of laughter, secrets nursed.

Pets parade and children prance,
While adults share a knowing glance.
The silliness we dare to plot,
Hidden tales that can't be caught.

When shadows leap and curtains sway,
Comedies of love at play.
Cups of tea and messy bites,
Turns into chic gala nights.

In corners where the sunbeams fall,
Muffled chuckles, over all.
Oh, what mischief costumes weave,
As fabric dreams and laughs conceive.

Unseen Conversations

Eavesdropping on mundane affairs,
Frogs and lizards in fancy glares.
Tales of dinner gone askew,
An opera sung by the cat in blue.

In hushed tones they plot and scheme,
While coasters twist in a tipsy dream.
Hidden debates over crumbs galore,
A heist of snacks—who could want more?

The sofa bears its weight with pride,
As secrets flow like they won't hide.
Cushions become a fortress tall,
For parodies of life, enthralled.

Phantom voices through the air,
Meanings masked, but none the rare.
To those outside, it may seem bland,
Magic thrives in this silent land.

Veils of Domestic Serenity

A riot nestled in soft frames,
Amidst the stillness, all are games.
Dust bunnies dance to a funky beat,
While chaos tiptoes on tiny feet.

Serenity wraps each scuffed old chair,
But laughter bubbles from anywhere.
Socks that mate with such delight,
Equally fit for day or night.

The kettle whistles a merry tune,
As dishes plot a daring swoon.
A wild troupe of mismatched cups,
Strike a pose as the laughter erupts.

In this haven where quirks collide,
A rainbow of mishaps shall abide.
To others, a peaceful, lifeless scene,
But here it bursts with jests obscene.

The Stillness Beneath the Drapes

Statuesque fluff in a grand display,
Bears witness to laughter's ballet.
While knock-knock jokes weave in the air,
The curtains giggle without a care.

Reflections prance with a flourish bright,
As shadows whisper, 'Oh, what a sight!'
The remote control's a royal scepter,
Commanding dramas of cats and masters.

Contentment reigns in mismatched socks,
While ticklish feet play silly knocks.
What lies beneath each tangled sheet?
Mirthful murmurs don't dare retreat.

Silent roars of humor pack tight,
Gales of joy in this cozy bite.
Where every giggle is a star,
Beneath these folds, we go far.

The Softness of Unspoken Words

There's a cat in a sunbeam, making a fuss,
While I sip my coffee, not wanting to blush.
She pounces on dust motes, the queen of her realm,
Making me chuckle, she's driving the helm.

A sock on the floor, a treasure, it seems,
The dog at the door has the weirdest of dreams.
He barks at the shadows, foes in the night,
But really it's just the moon's silly light.

The plant's in a corner, looking quite grumpy,
Wishing for water, or maybe a puppy.
It talks to the wall, a secret it keeps,
While I giggle softly before I fall asleep.

Carrots in aprons and sweaters so bright,
In my kitchen they're dancing, what a silly sight!
I laugh with the laughter that fills up this space,
This room is a circus; life's not a race.

Portals to the Forgotten Moments

A dusty old frame holds a time in the past,
When my uncle slipped on a rug, oh, the laugh!
We all stood in shock, then burst into cheer,
Those moments are golden, they sparkle and steer.

A toy train chugs softly, it's stuck in the fray,
As it loops 'round the table, it won't go away.
The laughter erupts, it's a sight to behold,
As the dog steals the cookies, so daring, so bold.

The curtains, they flutter, with secrets they keep,
A ghost in the armchair, pretending to sleep.
Grandma swears she saw him, she thinks he just snores,
But we know he's just hiding with snacks and some roars.

A recipe written with flour on the floor,
Tells tales of the times we forgot to ignore.
Each slip, every spill, gets a giggle and sigh,
Who knew life could somersault and cause us to fly?

Whispers of the Quiet Space

In the hush of a moment, a chair starts to creak,
Is it ghosts of my snacks or the cat trying to sneak?
I watch with delight as the popcorn takes flight,
Like confetti in silence, it steals all the night.

The clock on the wall has a tick-tock parade,
It dances with shadows, a quirky charade.
The cats hold a council, plotting their schemes,
With thoughts that are wild, like their culinary dreams.

A sofa that swallows, where crumbs seem to thrive,
It whispers of secrets that help me survive.
With laughter and giggles, the mirth fills the air,
Crafted from joy, oh, there's nothing to compare.

In each silent moment that tickles my mind,
I find bits of mischief that life's oft combined.
The quiet can hum with the joy that it brings,
With whispers and chuckles, oh the joy of small things!

Shadows of a Hidden World

A shadowy figure in the corner just blinked,
Could it be my slipper, or is it just ink?
It shuffles, it giggles, with laughter quite sly,
As I ponder in mystery, oh my, oh my!

Behind the old couch lies a monster, they say,
Of crumbs and old socks, it wants them to stay.
It grumbles and mumbles, a creature of lore,
We laugh at its antics, never a bore.

The curtains are swaying with tales left unsaid,
Like a puppet in a play where everyone's wed.
We join in the jest, with a wink and a cheer,
For shadows and laughter coalesce far and near.

The world is a funhouse, where absurdity reigns,
Every giggle and snort pulls us back in the lanes.
So hide and seek laughter in corners of life,
For joy is the journey amidst the strife.

Cracked Spines of Tales Untold

Books stacked high, a tower of dreams,
Whispers of stories in sunlight beams.
Cats plot mischief on pages worn,
Chasing shadows, or maybe a horn.

A cup of tea spills on the floor,
While giggles erupt, oh what a chore!
The dog looks guilty, as he should,
He was just trying to fetch the good.

Old chairs creak with tales untold,
Fables of laughter, mishaps bold.
A slice of cake mysteriously gone,
The crumbs on the couch sing a song.

Grandma's knitting in a fuzzy trance,
Knots and stitches that start to dance.
The patterns twist, they turn and weave,
In this circus of comforts, we believe.

The Pulse of Domesticity

The clock ticks softly, a rhythmic tune,
While socks discover the strength of the moon.
Plants debate whether to grow or wait,
In the sun's glow, they cultivate fate.

A vacuum hums a dancing jig,
While lost remote plays hide and seek big.
The fridge whispers secrets of last night's feast,
As leftovers plot their dinner time beast.

Neighbors wonder about our mess,
Pancake battles that caused distress.
With spatulas held like swords in hand,
We celebrate chaos, oh isn't it grand?

Kids cycle round in quick abandon,
Poetry sprawls where they usually stand.
In this heartbeat of home, smiles abound,
Life's funny flips keep us all unbound.

Fleeting Moments in Scenic Frames

Frames hang crooked, a little askew,
Memories frozen, some vibrant and blue.
A moment captured, yet so absurd,
The cat in a hat, it's truly unheard!

Coffee spills over a love note's edge,
While plants argue over the couch's ledge.
Caught in snapshots, a giggle, a cry,
Time playfully whispers, oh my, oh my!

Socks carry secrets of hasty retreats,
While dust bunnies gather for curious feats.
Each picture tells tales of joy and plight,
In this zany gallery, life feels just right.

A burst of laughter, a tiny parade,
Bringing the mundane to beautiful shade.
In the fleeting moments, we find our fame,
So many quirks in this wild lifetime game.

Echoes of Sighs and Smiles

A distant echo calls for a snack,
While the couch leaves us a cushy track.
Laugh lines deepen as stories unfold,
In the quiet chaos, we warm the cold.

The toaster pops, breakfast in flight,
As cereal renegades take on the night.
Teaspoons jive in a porcelain dance,
Biscuit crumbs scatter in a clumsy prance.

Pillows conspire to catch our dreams,
Soft whispers of nonsense, or so it seems.
Chuckles escaping from corners unseen,
In this merry bedlam, we've all been keen.

Through sighs that spiral and smiles that gleam,
Home is a canvas painted with cream.
In laughter and warmth, our stories collide,
Joyfully crafted, with hearts open wide.

Fleeting Footsteps and Dust Motions

Invisible paws on polished floors,
A dance of dust where laughter soars.
Forgotten socks hiding with grace,
In a game where we all lose the race.

The cat's a phantom, sneaky and sly,
Pouncing on shadows that flit on by.
Crumbs of cookies like treasure trails,
Echoes of giggles that never fail.

The clock ticks loud, a playful tease,
While we're all lost in comfy ease.
Fleeting moments wrapped in warmth,
As sneaky dust claims its own charm.

Peeking just slightly, a curious eye,
A dance of life as the day goes by.
And though we giggle, we sometimes sigh,
For this slice of joy, how time can fly.

A Tapestry of Familiarity

Threads of chatter weave through the air,
As the couch embraces each gentle stare.
Shenanigans blossom, like flowers in spring,
In this vibrant place where the heart takes wing.

The corner holds secrets, like whispers so sweet,
While popcorn confetti cushions our feet.
Each stained-old cushion a relic of joy,
Holding laughter and tears of every girl and boy.

The TV flickers, a familiar friend,
With jokes that seem to never end.
We giggle and gasp at the antics we see,
Wrapped in our warmth, just you and me.

In this tapestry spun with threads of cheer,
Comfy confessions we gladly share here.
With memories stitched in each playful glance,
We twirl through life in a joyous dance.

Murmurs of Mirth and Melancholy

Echoes of laughter twist with a sigh,
In this sanctuary where time floats by.
The quilted silence dances with light,
As day turns slowly to embrace the night.

A joker in shadows, a tickle of doubt,
Yet smirks and giggles come swirling about.
Moments collide like a fleeting kiss,
In this realm of laughter, what do we miss?

There's a sock on the coffee table's bough,
A head-scratching mystery, I wonder how!
With each silly grin and friendly tease,
Life brings its own crumbs, like a gentle breeze.

As night draws near, our stories entwine,
The murmurs of life are both yours and mine.
In the echo of joy, a bittersweet song,
We hold on tight, and we sing along.

The Compass of Intimacy

In this cozy nook, where we quietly conspire,
One nudge, a wink, and we light the fire.
Companions in chaos, yet calm like the sea,
We navigate laughter, just you and me.

The cushions conspire to share their tales,
Of socks that have wandered, and ice cream trails.
Every soft murmur becomes a refrain,
In this map of moments, pleasure and pain.

Our chatter like stars that twinkle and glow,
Mapping the moments, the high and the low.
A compass of secrets laid out on the floor,
Where every funny story opens a door.

In this playful maze, we stumble and tread,
With chuckles that bounce in the space overhead.
And though time is fleeting, our joy stays fine,
In this compass of closeness, your hand in mine.

www.ingramcontent.com/pod-product-compliance
Lightning Source LLC
Chambersburg PA
CBHW051731290426
43661CB00122B/220